CU01163384

Original title:
Lemon Pies and Sweet Vibes

Copyright © 2025 Creative Arts Management OÜ
All rights reserved.

Author: Sebastian Whitmore
ISBN HARDBACK: 978-1-80586-330-4
ISBN PAPERBACK: 978-1-80586-802-6

Honeyed Breezes and Zesty Scenes

In a land where laughter roams free,
Joyful fruits hang from each tree.
The sun winks down with a cheeky grin,
Flavorful mischief, let the fun begin!

Tickling taste buds with every bite,
Sugary tangs that feel just right.
Dancing ants in a playful spree,
Gather 'round, come share with me!

Sweet Whirls in Sunlit Skies

Round and round in a dizzy delight,
Creamy swirls on a warm summer night.
The bees are buzzing a jolly tune,
While we laugh and chase the fading moon.

Twists of flavor in each dainty slice,
A giggling feast, oh, how nice!
Butterfly laughter fills the air,
As sugary dreams float everywhere!

Nostalgic Citrus Symphony

Childhood memories of sun-soaked days,
Sippers and giggles in playful ways.
Every bite a burst of a sunny cheer,
Each tart note brings the past near.

With splashes of joy and a zestful twist,
How could we ever resist?
Lemonade laughter in every dish,
Sweetened nostalgia, how we wish!

A Mellow Breeze of Flavor

Sailing softly on a breezy lift,
Tasting the sunshine, a delectable gift.
Every slice a reason to clink our cups,
With silly cheers and joyful hiccups.

Sugar rushes and giggles abound,
In this fruity realm, happiness found.
So take a seat, come on, don't be shy,
Let's savor the moment and let out a sigh!

Slices of Joyful Reflection

In the sun, a tart delight,
Beneath the cloud of fluffy white.
Crust crumbling, laughter swirls,
As zest of life unfurls.

A pie in hand, the world seems bright,
Each bite, a giggle, pure delight.
Sour and sweet, a dance divine,
With every fork, a moment shines.

Golden Crumbs of Wonder

Golden treasures on the plate,
Whisking dreams, oh isn't fate?
Tales of joy in every slice,
A sprinkle of laughter, oh so nice.

Whirled up memories, flaky flair,
Biting into love and care.
With crumbs that spread a smile so wide,
In each piece, the giggles glide.

The Art of Zesty Indulgence

Dancing zest in buttery art,
A pinch of joy, a dimpled heart.
With every nibble, jokes resound,
In the kitchen, laughter's found.

Whipped cream clouds, a laughter spree,
Spoons clinking, oh so carefree.
Colors bright, a blissful sight,
Every slice, a silly bite.

Treasures from the Oven

In the warmth of cozy nooks,
Magic brews in recipe books.
Bubbly sweetness, tales unfold,
A warm embrace, a pie of gold.

Jokes rise up with every crust,
In flavors rich, we place our trust.
Filling hearts with joyfulness,
Every slice a sweet caress.

Citrus Rhapsody on a Fork

A zesty dance on my plate,
With a splash of sunshine fate.
Whispers of tartness in the air,
Send giggles up to the fair.

Balmy sweetness in a crust,
Oh, this flavor, I must trust!
Every forkful sparks delight,
As joy bubbles, oh so bright.

Glazed Delights in Gentle Breezes

A shimmer calls with every bite,
Underneath this warm sunlight.
Smiles are served with a dollop,
Wobbly happiness to top.

A dance of cream, a subtle tease,
This merry treat aims to please.
With crust so flaky, light as air,
Laughter mingles everywhere.

Hertz of Happiness in Every Bite

With each taste, a giggle escapes,
Silly flavors, funny shapes.
Zingy curd, a playful swing,
Melodies of joy they bring.

In every layer, secrets hide,
A surprise in each bite, side by side.
Sugar sprinkles like falling stars,
Tickling tongues from near and far.

A Tarte of Whimsy and Wonder

Crisp edges flaunt their charm,
A dessert that makes hearts warm.
Whimsy drizzled on top, you see,
   Crowning a slice of jubilee.

Beneath each layer, joy resides,
Upside-down these flavors glide.
With each fork, a chuckle blooms,
   As happiness sweetly looms.

Tangy Dreams in a Sugar Crust

In a world where zests collide,
Sugar dances on the side.
A crust that cracks with joyous cheer,
Dreams of citrus whisper near.

Mirthful spritz in every bite,
Tartness shines, a pure delight.
Giggles rise with every fork,
Brightening smiles as we all smirk.

Citrus Serenade at Dusk

When the sun dips low and bright,
Zesty notes take graceful flight.
Frothy laughter spills around,
In citrus songs, joy is found.

The twilight hints at laughter's sway,
While crumbs and giggles gently play.
Kooky flavors take their stand,
In evening's joy, we all demand.

Golden Slices of Joy

Golden slices with flair and sway,
Dancing on a counter tray.
Each bite brings a silly squeal,
As sweetness wraps like a surreal meal.

Crumbly laughter fills the room,
With every slice, the happiness blooms.
Let's toss our forks in pure delight,
And share our jokes 'til late at night.

The Flavors of Happiness

In a patch of radiant zest,
Whisked together, we are blessed.
Tickles from the sugary layer,
Crafting giggles that don't betray her.

With every spoonful, delight unfolds,
Tales of fun and joy retold.
Each tart twist brings us a grin,
In flavors where the laughter spins.

Crusts of Happiness Wrapped with Care

Golden crusts line the plate,
Joyful smiles anticipate fate.
Fluffy mounds, a sight to behold,
Zesty bites, stories unfold.

Whisking up giggles and cheer,
As we savor, the flavors steer.
A dance of sweetness, a lighthearted chase,
In every forkful, pure bliss we taste.

Laughter Served Warm and Zesty

Sprinkle some joy with a pinch of glee,
A tarty twist, just wait and see.
The warmth of the oven, a playful embrace,
Each slice we serve, a grin on each face.

Crusts that crumble with a soft, sweet sigh,
Bubbly laughter, like clouds in the sky.
Every bite, a giggle so bright,
Who knew such nonsense could taste just right?

A Fest of Flavorful Luminescence

Dancing flavors in every slice,
A sassy zing, oh so nice.
Chasing shadows, we feast in delight,
With laughter that echoes late into night.

Citrusy charms sprinkled all around,
In this wild party, joy is unbound.
With every forkful, a tale to share,
Bright moments crafted, beyond compare.

Sweet Zest Under Moonlight

Under the glow of the bright moon,
A tart dance begins, oh so soon.
Zesty laughs fill the starry air,
Laughter like sugar, light without care.

Crusts that crinkle, a playful tease,
Bouncing around, they aim to please.
With each bite, a giggle escapes,
Tiny explosions, like candy capes.

Taste of Childhood in Each Bite

Remember those days, oh what a blast,
Sticky fingers, the fun never passed.
With crumbs on our shirts and smiles so wide,
Flavorful joy, there's nowhere to hide.

Each slice took us back, oh what a ride,
Like joy-filled kites dancing in the tide.
A splash of nostalgia, a sprinkle of cheer,
Each morsel relived every memory dear.

Glimmering Sugar and Bright Splendor

Glimmers of sugar, a sweet cascade,
Rays of delight, in layers arrayed.
Wobbly wonders on plates adorned,
A sugary feast where laughter is born.

With every slice, a giggling cheer,
Echoed delight, so sweet and clear.
Frosting that twirls like a dancer's spree,
In this sugary realm, we all feel free.

A Whimsy of Flavors

In the land of flavors, oh what a show,
Juggling tastes like a circus pro.
Swirls of tang and whimsy unite,
A festival of laughter, pure delight.

When friends gather round with forks in hand,
It's a playful feast, oh so grand.
With bites that tickle and joy that bursts,
In this world of flavor, laughter thirsts.

Whimsy in a Whipped Cloud

Fluffy clouds float high in the sky,
Where giggles and grins decide to fly.
A dollop of joy in every bite,
Tasting the fun in pure delight.

Custard dreams swirl in a dance,
Promises of laughter in every glance.
A sprinkle of giggles and hints of glee,
Clouds of cream, oh what a spree!

Tarty faces with playful grins,
In a world where every slice wins.
Sweet dreams linger on the tongue,
As the air is filled with songs unsung.

Slices of Joy on a Silver Platter

Round and round the table spins,
With flavors and laughter, where fun begins.
Each cut reveals a savory tale,
Of jests and quips that never pale.

A silver platter shines with cheer,
Each slice a giggle, far and near.
Whisked up laughter in every taste,
No time for frowns, there's fun to waste!

The zest of life, a tangy twist,
Mixing joy that can't be missed.
With every forkful, we share a smile,
Filling our hearts with zestful style.

Laughter Flavored with Zest

Jokes are served with a citrus twist,
In a world of laughter, it can't be missed.
A scoop of fun, a hint of flair,
Tickled taste buds floating in the air.

Crisp bites burst with joy so bright,
Each chuckle adds to the pure delight.
Flavors fizzle and friends unite,
As we savor every playful bite.

Bright Bites of Happiness

Sunshine spills on every plate,
With every bite, we celebrate.
Joyful moments come alive,
As we gather, chuckling, we thrive.

Tiny bursts of cheerful cheer,
Sparking joy when friends are near.
Each laugh, a nibble full of fun,
Baking memories, everyone!

Zesty Comes the Day

Wake up, sunshine, bring on the cheer,
A tart little treat, it's finally here!
Whisking and mixing, oh what a sight,
Smiles are baking; everything's right.

Laughter's a sprinkle, a dash of delight,
With giggles and grins, we'll party all night.
Citrus eruptions, a playful parade,
Every sweet slice, a joyful charade.

Happiness Baked to Perfection

Golden crusts and fillings so bright,
Every bite bursts with pure delight.
Whipped cream fluff, a cloud on my plate,
Mirth in each morsel; isn't it great?

Who needs a reason? Just grab a fork,
Join in the fun, let smiles uncork!
Silly puns dancing, oh what a bliss,
Each slice a hug, in buttery kiss.

Sweet Joys Beneath the Stars

Under the moonlight, we gather our friends,
With treats in hand, the laughter never ends.
Filling our hearts with sugary dreams,
Laughter and sweetness blend at the seams.

Sipping on breezes, the night's just begun,
With zany toppings, we've already won.
Jokes as zesty as the flavors we share,
In this delightful night, there's humor to spare.

Citrus Glow in the Morning

Morning arrives with a zesty surprise,
The sunbeams are bright, much like our pies.
Mixing and stirring, oh what a scene,
In this cheerful chaos, we reign as the queen!

Slather on giggles, sprinkle on fun,
With every creation, we've already won.
Mornings are magic, with treats piled high,
Joy rises early, and so does our pie.

Dappled Light and Delightful Bites

In the kitchen, chaos reigns,
A whisk and giggles, no one complains.
Batter splatters, flour clouds bloom,
A tasting spoon fights for more room.

Zesty laughter fills the air,
Lemon drops tumble everywhere.
Cookies dance, oh what a sight,
In this merry baking light.

Sweets of the Sunlit Garden

Bumblebees buzz in the sun,
Mixing up fun, oh what a run!
Butterflies hop from cake to grass,
Getting royally silly, oh what a sass!

With fruit parade on the outdoor table,
Every bite's a joy when we're able.
Giggles erupt with every taste,
In this jolly, scrumptious haste.

A Dance of Cream and Citrus

Sugar swirls, a dreamy sight,
Creamy dreams take flavored flight.
Spoons collide with playful cheers,
A whipped-top battle, oh my dears!

Cartwheeling zest skips on the floor,
MischIEF in the mix, who could ask for more?
Silly faces and frosting smears,
Creating memories, bursting with cheers.

Sunshine's Kiss on Tasty Crusts

Golden crusts like sunbeams gleam,
Chasing every giggling dream.
Each slice served with a cheeky grin,
A playful tug, let the fun begin!

Sparklers lit in every bite,
Fill the air with pure delight.
As laughter echoes, joy will rise,
In this feast under sunny skies.

A Slice of Sunbeam

In the kitchen, a dance of zesty flair,
A citrus fling, with laughter in the air.
Whipped cream spirals, a playful delight,
Crusts crumbling softly, a joyous sight.

Sunshine in each bite, a giggle or two,
A forkful of fun, and a sprinkle of goo.
Sour meets sweet in a jubilant race,
Smiles bubbling over—oh, what a place!

Whirlwind of Taste and Light

A twirl of flavor, a burst of cheer,
Zest on my tongue, happiness near.
With every forkful, a ticklish tease,
A confection of mirth that brings me to knees.

Crumble and giggle, a tangy parade,
In a world of delight, all woes seem to fade.
Life's little whispers wrapped in a crust,
Savor each moment; oh, how I must!

Crusty Echoes of Laughter

Chatter and clatter, the oven's warm glow,
Sliced joy on a platter, a rambunctious show.
Giggles on the edges, sweetness in the core,
With each playful bite, I just want more!

Sticky fingers and crumbs dance 'round the floor,
Joyful explosions, let's all shout for more!
A crumbly riddle, a taste of delight,
In this whirlwind of joy, everything feels right.

Frosted Memories with a Twist

Whipped to perfection, a dollop of fun,
Twisted tales linger, under the sun.
Each layer a chuckle, each bite a reprise,
Wit wrapped in frosting, a sweet surprise.

With every bright forkful, nostalgia will bloom,
Scent of the citrus, filling the room.
A treat for the senses, a party unfurled,
In laughter and sweetness, we twirl through the world.

Savory Echoes of Citrus Bliss

In a kitchen bright and bold,
Citrus tales are often told.
A zesty twist that makes us grin,
Laughter bubbles from within.

With forks that dance and twirl around,
A flavor fight, such joy is found.
We mix and mash with silly cheer,
Citrus dreams that draw us near.

Unexpected laughter rings so true,
As frosting flies and faces stew.
A bite of joy that makes us sing,
In the kitchen, chaos is our king.

So come and join this fruity brawl,
Where every morsel leads to downfall.
With silly hats and aprons tight,
We savor joy, our silly plight.

Fancy Crusts and Fanciful Days

Roll the dough and make it dance,
With flour flying, all in a trance.
A pinch of whimsy, a dollop of fun,
In this bake-off, we've already won.

The crust is crisp, a golden hue,
With every slice, more laughter grew.
Spinning stories while mixing zest,
A culinary game of jest and fest.

Whipped cream clouds that float on top,
As giggles double with every plop.
We aim for sweet but land on silly,
In this kitchen, fun grows frilly.

A sprinkle here, a swirl of cream,
In our world, we live the dream.
With every bite, a chuckle shared,
Fancy treats, but really, we've fared.

A Palette of Sunny Flavors

Colors burst on every plate,
A citrus splash, oh isn't it great?
With every bite, we jump and sway,
In this feast, we laugh away.

Taste buds dancing with a zing,
As giggles rise and joy takes wing.
We dive into the zestful swirl,
In this kitchen, we all twirl.

Unexpected flavors bump and glide,
With jokes that blossom like the tide.
A splash of fun to light the day,
In sweet delight, we laugh and play.

So gather 'round for tasty cheer,
With every slice, we hold dear.
A party bright with flavors bold,
In every laugh, the tales are told.

Whimsical Whirls of Sweetness

Twist and twirl, we whip the cream,
In a whirl of fun, we all gleam.
Silly hats on every head,
With laughter shared, our worries shed.

Sugary swirls that make us laugh,
In every bite, we share a gaff.
Rolling dough like it's a game,
With every mishap, we stake our claim.

A dash of zest, a splash of cheer,
In this baking spree, we persevere.
Giggles echo while mixing bright,
As sweetness reigns and moods ignite.

So come along and taste the joy,
In every slice, we find our ploy.
With every giggle, our hearts do sing,
In whimsical worlds, our joy takes wing.

Bright Morsels of Bliss

In a baking spree, oh what a sight,
Giggles rise with each doughy bite.
Whiskers of cream on the nose do dwell,
Baking blunders, oh do tell!

Sugar sprinkles like confetti in air,
Muffins dancing without a care.
A pop of zest, a splash of cheer,
Who knew flour could bring such beer?

Every crust tells a funny tale,
A pinch of chaos, we never fail.
Cherries wobble like jellybeans,
On the counter, hilarious scenes!

So grab a fork and join the fun,
The laughter rises, we've just begun.
Bright morsels await, so don't be shy,
Let happiness crust, come on, oh my!

Juicy Fantasies in the Bakery

In the bakery's glare, life swells with joy,
Banana peels danced with a baker's toy.
Cupcakes giggle, sprinkles collide,
In this nutty world, we take a wild ride!

Rooftops of frosting and dreams so grand,
Each slice unveils a wonderland.
Icing drips, oh what a plight,
A sugary mess, what a delight!

Rolling pins in silly haste,
Cookies pop out, in a sugar-laced chase.
Tarts strut with flair, oh what a scheme,
In this fruity realm, we live the dream!

So, grab your aprons, let's bake away,
With juicy romance in the food ballet.
Laughter in the kitchen fuels the fire,
Whisking fun into our sweet desire!

Sunkissed Sweetness

Under the sun, cakes shine so bright,
Whipped cream dreams in the golden light.
Berries tumble with giggles anew,
Sweeter than honey, life's a big brew!

The oven hums a quirky tune,
Doughnuts dancing like it's June.
Sunbeams mingle with frosted treats,
While sugar ants prance on little feasts!

Every bite a joyful surprise,
Chasing memories beneath the skies.
Creating chaos? Oh, what a thrill,
A pudding splat will fit the bill!

So take a seat and enjoy the show,
With flavors that sparkle and giggles that flow.
Sunkissed delights in a colorful spree,
Let's whip up mischief, just you and me!

Curves of Flavor and Fun

Whipped cream clouds with a hint of zing,
A cartwheel of flavors, let joy take wing.
Swirls and twirls in the mixing bowl,
With every batter, we unleash the soul!

Cheesecake chimed with a zany grin,
A twist of the lemon makes chaos begin.
Bakers laugh 'til they fall on the floor,
With every sprinkle, they shout for more!

Crispy edges and gooey delight,
Sugar highs carry us through the night.
We build our dreams with love and some mess,
In this odd kitchen, it's pure happiness!

So come and join this whimsical race,
With curves of flavor, we pick up the pace.
In our lovely bakery, we'll dance and run,
For life's a treat, let's have some fun!

Slices of Happiness

When life hands you fruit, take a bite,
A giggle escapes, what pure delight.
Sugar dusted smiles, oh so bright,
The joy of the bake, a scrumptious sight.

Whisking away worries, mixing with glee,
A dash of whimsy, just wait and see.
Pies cooling off, they dance with the breeze,
A sweet little tune, that brings us to ease.

Fill the plate high, let flavors collide,
With laughter and joy, they can't be denied.
Grinning so wide, like kids in a fair,
Each forkful a treasure, beyond compare.

So grab a slice, and let worries go,
It's time to indulge, in the warmth of the glow.
A gathering of friends, let the fun ignite,
With every sweet bite, everything feels right.

Golden Curves of Delight

Round and golden, oh what a scene,
Shiny and bright, like a sunbeam.
Crusts that wave, with a flaky embrace,
These enchanting treats bring smiles to each face.

Gather around, let's take a peek,
At gooey goodness, it's rather unique.
Filling our hearts with laughter and cheer,
As we dig into flavors, we hold so dear.

No pie left behind, that's our decree,
Slicing and sharing, so carefree.
Each bite's a giggle, a festive parade,
In this playful kitchen, memories are made.

So savor each moment, as we toast,
To golden delights, we love the most.
With forks high in the air, let joy ignite,
In this pie-loving world, everything feels right.

Citrus Bliss and Creamy Dreams

Zesty whispers in a buttery shell,
A flavor explosion, can't you tell?
Creamy swirls, like a tale told bright,
In every sweet bite, there's pure delight.

Sprinkling happiness, a sprinkle or two,
Joyful giggles in the kitchen crew.
Flip the spatula, dance with the dough,
A riot of flavors, putting on a show.

Creamy clouds swirl on top with flair,
Bubbling laughter fills the air.
Each slice a party, beneath a sunny deck,
With chuckles and crumbs, what the heck!

So come on over, let's slice and share,
We'll plunge into laughter, without a care.
Satiating cravings, while music plays,
In this world of sweetness, we bask all day.

A Taste of Summer's Kiss

Sunshine captured in every spoon,
A burst of joy, like a lively tune.
Jubilant flavors tickle the tongue,
With every fresh slice, feel forever young.

Sizzling laughter in a picnic spread,
Where crumbs and stories gently tread.
Ice cream drips, like giggles so sweet,
What fun to devour this sunny treat!

Gather your friends, it's a carnival call,
With vibrant colors that enchant us all.
Each bite a memory, a festive embrace,
In the realm of fun, we claim our space.

No frowns allowed, just laughter and cheer,
With every sweet slice, we conquer our fears.
So let's celebrate with zest and bliss,
For life is a pie, let's relish this kiss.

Cheery Flavors of Joy

In the kitchen, laughter rings bright,
Mixing zests with a dash of delight.
Silly faces and sticky hands,
Sweet treats made in our goofy plans.

The oven hums a happy tune,
Bouncing around like a dancing cartoon.
Giggles spill like sugar on floors,
Flavors burst through the open doors.

Crusts that crumble, filling so grand,
Makes us feel like a rockstar band.
Whipped cream clouds swirl in the air,
Creating joy without a care.

Little bites bring the sunshine in,
Every nibble, a laugh, where to begin?
With each fork full, we share the cheer,
It's a funny feast, my friends, oh dear!

Sunlit Dreams and Tasty Whirls

Under the sun, we create a scene,
Baking wonders where giggles convene.
Spoonfuls flying, we twirl and spin,
Sweet dreams unfold, let the fun begin.

Chasing each other round and about,
With splashes of cream, there's no room for doubt.
Dough squishes snug between our toes,
In this kitchen, anything goes.

Colors popping, a vibrant delight,
Cakes that shimmer in the golden light.
Every slice, a joy to behold,
Tales of laughter and treasures retold.

With every bake, we draft a new song,
A symphony of flavors, where we belong.
Sunlit moments, we savor and twirl,
In our sweet world, let the laughter furl.

Sunshine on My Palette

A dash of sunshine, a sprinkle of cheer,
Bright colors splash, it's my favorite sphere.
Gathering smiles, we mix and blend,
Creating sunshine, the sweetest trend.

In bowls of joy, the ingredients dance,
Whisking up memories, giving them a chance.
Our giggles rise like a perfect meringue,
In this playful place, our hearts sang.

Frosting swirls like a rainbow's embrace,
With candy jewels, we brighten the space.
Each tasty bite, a giggly delight,
Leaving behind a trail of pure light.

In this canvas, fun colors arise,
Crafting laughter in humble supplies.
Signature flavors, a festival grand,
Savoring moments, hand in hand.

Zesty Whispers of Delight

Bursts of zesty fun fill the air,
In the kitchen, each silly stare.
Mixing ingredients with playful flair,
A comic delight that's beyond compare.

Sticky fingers from fruity splashes,
Laughter erupts in sugary clashes.
Every dollop, a wink and a nod,
In our sweet chaos, we all applaud.

Crusty surprises and gooey spills,
A blend of dreams with a sprinkle of thrills.
Flavor explosions, what a delight,
In our candy kitchen, joy takes flight.

Serving up giggles with every slice,
A recipe crafted, oh so nice.
With every taste, we sing and cheer,
In this zesty life, we persevere!

Zingy Sunshine and Warm Embrace

A smile so bright, it pierces the gloom,
With zestful laughs that brighten the room.
Tickling tongues with a fruity cheer,
Let's savor the joy, and give a loud cheer!

Silly giggles bounce off the wall,
Like citrus bursts at a rambunctious call.
Every slice brings a dance to our feet,
With flavors that spark, oh, what a treat!

Whisking together all things divine,
In a swirl of colors, oh, how they shine!
Biting into light, sweetness unfolds,
As happiness glimmers, the laughter holds.

So come on friends, let's raise our glass,
To flavors so bold, let's make this last.
Souring woes with a joyful surprise,
In the warmth of friendship, our spirits rise.

Sweets Beneath the Blossom

In a garden where giggles flutter and play,
Sweets bloom wildly on a bright spring day.
Petal-soft whispers of fruit-filled delights,
Dance in the breeze, oh what appetites!

Crusts crumbling lightly like laughter in air,
With sweetened aromas that swirl everywhere.
Beneath the boughs of carefree delight,
We munch on the joy until late in the night.

As we chase after sunshine with fork in our hands,
Tasting the joy that each morsel expands.
Silly faces smeared with sugary grace,
In this treat-filled wonder, we all find our place.

So let's raise a toast to the crumbs on the floor,
To the giggles and grins, who could ask for more?
With every sweet nibble, we share our own whim,
In the blossom of laughter, let's all take a swim.

Tangy Nights and Sugary Mornings

Morning awakens with a tangy surprise,
A playful swirl twirls before our eyes.
With each bite, a chuckle, a giggle takes flight,
As sparks of sweetness dance in the light.

Evening rolls in with a cheeky grin,
Choosing to join in the flavor-filled spin.
With pies on the table, a riot of taste,
Each slice we devour, let's not let it waste!

Fruit-filled dreams tease in the soft evening glow,
As whispers of laughter around us now flow.
Bringing together both friends and delight,
Under tangy stars, our spirits take flight.

So here's to the fun, let's savor it slow,
With sugary moments and giggles that grow.
For each bite we take is a memory churned,
In nights rich with laughter, the sweetness is earned.

Citrus Drizzle Over Smiles

Under the sky dappled with laughter and glee,
A drizzle of zest makes all of us free.
Smiles are brewing in flavors so bright,
Each taste a giggle that lights up the night.

Tables adorned with a sunshine glow,
As flavors combine in a tantalizing show.
Sticky fingers passing around each delight,
While chuckles and banter take joyful flight.

Each bite drizzles happiness, nothing is bland,
With citrusy twists, we all take a stand.
Sharing the moments, a jest in the fare,
Together we flourish, a flavor affair.

So let's fill our hearts with this bubbling joy,
As laughter and pie become every girl's toy.
In every bright corner, with memories sweet,
Citrus smiles linger, so life feels complete.

Citrus Serenade

A tree swings ripe with citrus bliss,
Its fruits dangle, like a sunny kiss.
Squirrels dance in wild delight,
As they plot to steal the fruit by night.

Lemonade fountains sprout in town,
Where laughter spreads and never drowns.
Sunburned cheeks and sticky hands,
Life is sweeter than we planned.

Bakers in aprons sing a tune,
While juggling fruit like a circus boon.
A zesty pie, with crust so flaky,
Laughing with joy, we're going crazy.

In this fruity fest, we skip and slide,
With every chuckle, joy's amplified.
Under the sun, we make their day,
In our quirky, citrusy play.

Sugar-kissed Daydreams

A whimsically sweetened dream takes flight,
Where pastry swirls tease the appetite.
Sugar-coated wishes float on the breeze,
Tickling our noses like playful bees.

Beneath the branches, giggles ring,
As cake and cookies take to wing.
Tickle-tart tales of zestful glee,
Savor the laughs, let your heart be free.

Children chase skies, with arms stretched wide,
Determined to catch what the sun can't hide.
Frosting smiles and kitchen chats,
In this joy parade, no room for mats.

Every bite, a dance on the tongue,
Songs of sweetness forever sung.
In this frolic where flavor's the theme,
We're lost in our sugar-kissed dream.

Zesty Whispers of Joy

In a garden spun with zestful glee,
Laughter bubbles like soda, carefree.
Dancing shadows in the afternoon glow,
As flavors mingle and frolic below.

A whiff of zest, as friends convene,
Creating giggles with each lemon scene.
Bite into joy, taste the surprise,
Sour and sweet, a feast for the eyes.

Whipped cream clouds drift above our heads,
While pie crust battles the crumbs that spread.
Sassy bites cause a raucous cheer,
With each zestful whisper, the fun draws near.

Chasing each other in citrus delight,
Singing harmonies until the night.
In a world where smiles never fold,
We revel in stories that never get old.

Tart Sunshine in a Crust

Sunshine bursts with a tartened flair,
As laughter dances in fruity air.
A crust so flaky, it's fit for kings,
Wrapped in flavors that joyously sing.

Around the table, friends collide,
With forks like wands, we all confide.
Each slice a treasure to savor and share,
In this sweet realm, none shall despair.

Frothy sips and cheeky grins,
Sparks of joy ignite our skins.
In this gathering that feels so right,
We're conquering tartness with sheer delight.

As the sun sets on our crisp delight,
We toast to laughter that lasts all night.
With every crumb, our hearts are spun,
In a crust of joy, we've truly won.

Basking in Golden Tastes

A crust that hugs a treasure tight,
Filled with joy, oh what a sight!
Whipped cream clouds that tickle the nose,
Each slice a dance where laughter flows.

Spoons at the ready, it's time to dive,
With bites so bright, we come alive.
Giggling crumbs on a sunny plate,
In this sweet realm, there's no room for hate.

Echoes of Sweet Sunsets

Golden rays spill on gummy shores,
Tickling taste buds, who could ask for more?
Chasing the sun with a sugary cheer,
Life's a party, let's grab a beer!

Fluffy meringue clouds drift on by,
As we eat and laugh, oh my oh my!
Friends gather 'round with cheeks so chubby,
In this flavor fest, we're all feelin' bubbly.

Charmed with Tangy Whimsy

A swirl of zest that sings a tune,
While giggles float beneath the moon.
Forks dance happily on tart delight,
In this marvelous mix, all feels right.

With a giggle and a wink, we indulge,
A flavor fiesta, let's all be bulge!
Witty banter on a sunny day,
Happiness served in bright buffet.

Creamy Dreams in a Zesty Frame

In a world where treats are delightfully bold,
Each slice serves up stories untold.
Marshmallow fluff and a citrus twist,
Who could escape such a daring tryst?

Crusty adventures, crunching with glee,
Laughter erupts like bubbles in tea.
With every spoonful, joy we declare,
In this silly game, we've no time to spare!

Poolside Sweets and Sunlight

Baking treats under the blazing sun,
I drop a slice—oh, this could be fun!
Whipped cream clouds, a sprinkle of cheer,
Taste test time—who's brave, who's near?

Laughing as I chase the dog outside,
He snatches a crust and I try to hide.
Cooling off with splashes, giggles galore,
Sticky hands wave—who could ask for more?

Happy Tastes from Past Seasons

Remembering summers and their fruity glee,
Frost on my nose, what a sight to see!
Granny's recipe—both sweet and tart,
Each bite a joy, a work of art.

A food fight with icing? Let's start a trend!
Whipped cream wars, who will make amends?
We laugh till we soar, like kites in the sky,
Chasing those flavors, the days whiz by.

The Language of Sweet Cravings

Whispers of sugar dance in the air,
I glance at my friend, who knows I won't share.
Chocolate and cherries, a confectionery thrill,
A bite of happiness—oh, what a skill!

We're baking a story, each layer a rhyme,
Squeezed lemons and giggles make our hearts climb.
We sketch out our dreams with frosting and cheer,
Savoring laughter while the sunset draws near.

Sugarcoated Sunshine and Happiness

Mango swirl dreams on a sunny high,
Giggling at shadows as time whizzes by.
The pie crust crackles, a funny old tune,
Baking with joy 'neath the warm afternoon.

Dancing around with a spoon in hand,
Crafting sweet magic, oh isn't life grand?
Sprinkling smiles in every bright hue,
Flavors of happiness, just for me and you.

Sunbeam Flavors in Whipped Cream

A dollop of joy on my plate,
Whipped cream dances, oh, what fate!
Bright yellow smiles in every bite,
Sugar and giggles take their flight.

Jokes on the crust, so flaky and light,
Squeezed sunshine beams, oh what a sight!
With each forkful, laughter erupts,
Silly dreams in every scoop, it's nuts!

Chasing the zest, the tangy fun,
Chirping flavors, a flavor run!
Wobbly smiles as we dig right in,
Who knew dessert could make us grin?

Whipped up moods, oh so divine,
Sipping jokes like lemon-lime!
A party on the table, let's not stop,
For with each slice, we laugh and pop!

Caresses of Sugar and Citrus

On a plate where the giggles gleam,
A frosty fork makes dessert a dream!
With a squeeze of zest, the fun begins,
Laughter echoes; oh, the playful sins!

Curly whiskers of cream parade,
Dancing joy in a lemon cascade.
Every bite a joke, sweet and bright,
Tempting our senses, a silly delight.

Tickling tones of sugary bliss,
Let's twirl and swirl, never miss!
Each slice a smile, a zestful tease,
Fun-filled moments that aim to please.

Sipping on giggles, we toast the day,
Brighter than the sun's own ray!
With twinkling eyes, let's make some noise,
For smiles are made with silly joys!

In Tune with Tangy Delights

In a world where laughter sings,
Squeezed sunshine and whimsical things.
A crust so crunchy, the cream's a dream,
With every bite, we're on the beam!

Tickling tongues in a citrus tease,
Whipped cream clouds that aim to please.
Jokes in the air, laughter on the run,
Savoring sweetness, all in the fun.

Giggly forks and cozy bites,
With every layer, playful sights.
Silly faces through each tangy twist,
In this sweet realm, we can't resist.

Round and round, the flavors dance,
In a cozy kitchen, we take a chance.
So pull up a chair and share a smile,
For these sweet treats make life worthwhile!

Sunlit Revelry on a Plate

Bright rays captured in every slice,
Crust so crisp, it's pure paradise!
Sunshine dances with stars of sweet,
Bringing laughter with each tasty treat.

Squirting giggles, the tangy tease,
Melting hearts like the summer breeze.
Cream swirls like silly, carefree glee,
Taste buds in tune, oh so happy we!

Pies that shine like glittering jokes,
Sending flavors through giddy folks.
Forks are flying, time skips along,
In this slice of joy, we all belong.

Turquoise skies and joyful bells,
Each bite's a story that sweetly dwells.
With every taste, we paint our cheer,
A sunlit fiesta, let's give a cheer!

Mirthful Moments Meringued

A zesty world of laughter bright,
With citrus smiles, we take flight.
Whisking dreams in bowls so round,
Joyful giggles all around.

Tarts and tales, we mix with glee,
Sour faces? No, not we!
Sugar sprinkles on our frowns,
Turning grumps to happy clowns.

Baking is an art, they say,
We fling flour in a playful way.
Crusts that crumble, spirits soar,
In the kitchen, we laugh more.

Meringue clouds on the whisk we spin,
Chasing troubles, let the fun begin!
A slice of chaos, a dollop of cheer,
In our sugary realm, we find our gear.

Sweet Citrus Dreams Await

In a sunbeam's glow, we dance and sway,
Citrus giggles brightening the day.
Squeezing smiles from every zest,
Whipping up the world's best jest.

Cookies crumble, laughter spills,
A sprinkle of joy, a dash of thrills.
With every bite, we share a grin,
In this tangy fun, we all win.

Rolling dough like we roll with life,
Stirring sweetness amidst the strife.
Every forkful makes hearts soar,
In this bright kitchen, who could ask for more?

Dancing flour, a leap, a twirl,
Joyful chaos begins to unfurl.
With citrus cheer, we rise and shine,
In our playful world, all's divine.

Harvesting Joy in Every Slice

In a pie cradle, joy does reside,
Each slice a giggle, a playful ride.
We ripen laughter, fresh and sweet,
Pies and puns, our favorite treat.

Gathering smiles like fallen leaves,
Baking magic, oh how it weaves!
With forks in hand, we dive right in,
Each bite a blissful, cheeky grin.

Citrus dances on our tongues,
Playful tunes and funny songs.
With every crumb, a joke is told,
In our happy kitchen, hearts unfold.

Sunshine glows in every dish,
Creating laughter, that's our wish.
A pinch of joy, a twist of fate,
In this sweet harvest, we're never late.

Flour, Sugar, and Gleeful Whispers

Whispers of sweetness fill the air,
Flour ruffles, laughter everywhere.
We giggle softly, whisk and spin,
Creating treats where joy begins.

Sugar crystals in a playful glow,
Making memories with every dough.
Sprinkling joy like confetti bright,
In this fun feast, everything's right.

Baking blunders, oh what a sight,
Flipping desserts, pure delight!
With halos of meringue, we charm the crowd,
In this playful chaos, we laugh loud.

As ovens warm, our spirits rise,
In a swirl of joy, we claim the prize.
With each crispy line and zesty cheer,
In our baking tale, happiness is near.

Creamy Dreams Wrapped in Citrus

In a sunlit kitchen, laughter swirls,
A dance of flour as the mixer whirls.
Zesty kisses from a jar so bright,
Tickling taste buds with citrus delight.

A crust that giggles, with a crunch so bold,
Whispering secrets of sweetness untold.
With a wink and a smile, the jello jives,
It's a party of flavors where joy arrives.

Whipped cream tumbles like clouds from above,
Each bite is a hug, a sugary love.
Plates piled high with sunshine so fine,
Serving up happiness, one slice at a time.

Curled up on the sofa, we dig in deep,
Making memories that we'll always keep.
With laughter and crumbs scattered all around,
In this cozy chaos, happiness is found.

Sweetness Tangled in Time

A twist of citrus, a splash of cheer,
Time dances with flavors, bringing us near.
With giggles and crumbs, we taste the fun,
Each slice a memory, warm like the sun.

Whirls of zest play hide and seek,
In this playful kitchen, joy is at peak.
A crust so flaky, it wants to shout,
In the ballet of baking, no room for doubt.

As forks dive in, the laughter roars,
Spoonfuls of sweetness, we're craving more.
Sticky fingers and smiles so wide,
This scrumptious adventure, our favorite ride.

With time on our side and crumbs in our hair,
The giggly escapade leads us somewhere.
With a wink at dessert, the world feels right,
In this tangled treat, we bask in light.

Joy Served on a Flaky Crust

Crust so flaky, it sings a tune,
A bed for joy, beneath the moon.
Zesty wonders await, bright and bold,
In this happy kitchen, stories are told.

Whipped clouds rise, fluffy and grand,
A sprinkle of laughter adds a sweet hand.
Each slice a giggle, a dance on the plate,
In this symphony of flavors, we celebrate.

With a charming flick, the juiciness flows,
Each bite a surprise, a tickle that grows.
Gather the friends, let the feasting begin,
In this joyful kitchen, everyone wins!

Laughter echoes as forks dive in,
Chasing the sweetness, it's a delicious win.
With every crumb, our hearts feel light,
In the magic of sharing, everything's right.

Golden Delights in a Glass Jar

In gleaming jars, the sunshine resides,
Golden delights where happiness hides.
With sprigs of joy perched nicely on top,
Each scoop a treasure, a flavorful pop.

Twirling and swirling, the flavors collide,
A tasty adventure we can't let slide.
Laughter erupts with each playful taste,
In this world of sweetness, there's never a waste.

As spoons dive deep into gooey delight,
Cravings fulfilled, all worries take flight.
With jars becoming friends, we gather around,
In this banquet of bliss, pure joy is found.

The fun's in the sharing, the moments you crave,
Each golden delight making hearts brave.
With smiles and hugs, we toast to the jar,
In this scrumptious journey, we know who we are.

A Tapestry of Tasteful Whirls

A slice of sunshine on my plate,
Crusty edges that look so great.
With every bite, I twirl and spin,
A dance of flavors, let the fun begin!

Bouncing flavors, laughter rolls,
In the kitchen, I find my goals.
Whisking joy with every stir,
My happy heart begins to purr.

Sour meets sweet, a playful tease,
With every bite, I'm hard to please.
Giggles rise like fluffy meringue,
In this treat, my spirit sang!

A sprinkle of zest, a dash of cheer,
I serve it up with raucous cheer.
For every mood, there's a slice,
In my world, this pie's the spice!

Timeless Delights Crafted with Love

Whisking dreams in a bowl so wide,
A taste of magic, come take a ride.
Crust so flaky, it flirts with the air,
In the oven, a sweet affair!

Golden smiles and sugary laughs,
A slice for you, and one for your chaff.
Wobbly wonders, they dance and sway,
In every corner, joy finds its way!

Homemade wonders, with giggles galore,
Each slice we share opens a door.
Spoon in hand, we'll savor the fun,
A pie party for everyone!

Crafted with giggles, sprinkled with zest,
This culinary fire puts smiles to the test.
For every bite, memories we sow,
In this sweet kitchen, love's the show!

Celestial Treats for Happy Hearts

Baked like a comet, a pie in the sky,
Sweetness and laughter, oh my, oh my!
A galaxy of flavors, bright as the sun,
Each bite a journey, each fork a fun run!

Stars sprinkle joy with each creamy swirl,
A pie on the table makes my heart twirl.
Giggles orbit like planets in flight,
In this sweet cosmos, everything's right!

A scoop of delight, a splash of cheer,
The more I share, the more I endear.
With every slice, we gather near,
In the warmth of joy, we hold each dear!

Mirthful moments, a celestial feat,
With each joyful fork, we savor the heat.
For happiness served with a side of zest,
In this pie galaxy, we are all blessed!

Subtle Citrus Sparkles

A dash of zing on a plate so bright,
Twinkling flavors in morning light.
Bouncing laughter, a zesty cheer,
Each bite a sparkle, oh my dear!

Sipping sunshine, we swirl and sway,
With every slice, we chase clouds away.
Bubbling giggles, a fun little tease,
In the world of tastes, nothing can freeze!

A twist of joy in a creamy dream,
Glorious flavors, like a dancing beam.
With each crumb shared, we find our song,
In sugary smiles, we all belong!

Crafted with glee, it's never a bore,
A banquet of laughter, who could ignore?
With every nibble, our hearts ignite,
In this citrus dance, we feel so bright!

Vibrant Yellow Melodies

In a bowl of sunshine, we mix and we play,
Sugar dances lightly, brightening the day.
A twist of zesty laughter fills the air,
As giggles bubble over, sweet treats laid bare.

With every tart slice, a chorus we sing,
Frothy dreams served up, what joy do they bring?
Whirlwinds of flavor, in every small space,
Joyfully spinning, a pie-making race.

Citrus delight wraps us in its embrace,
Tickling our senses, no frown to replace.
Crusts crunch like crickets, while flavors collide,
In the vibrant dance, a delicious ride.

So grab a fork quickly, let laughter ignite,
With each silly bite, our hearts take flight.
Savoring chaos, life's quirky reprise,
In kitchens where humor and flavor arise.

Citrus Kisses Beneath the Stars

Under the twinkling, a sweet pie parade,
Citrus kisses bursting, never to fade.
Sugar-coated giggles, we savor the night,
As laughter and zests fill the world with delight.

Moonlight holds secrets of fluff on the side,
Where sticky fingers messily glide.
A tartness so playful, such fun it evokes,
In pastry-filled dreams, we tell silly jokes.

A sprinkle of joy with every bright bite,
Starlit confessions, our hearts feeling light.
With winks shared in whispers, a zest of surprise,
We cherish these moments, our sweet alibis.

So gather your friends, let the fun never cease,
In this pie-loving wonder, we find our peace.
Beneath the vast cosmos, we dance and we cheer,
With citrusy magic, we banish all fear.

Whipped Cream and Warm Embrace

A dollop of laughter atop a warm treat,
Whipped dreams floating high, our joy can't be beat.
Marshmallows giggle, all fluffy and white,
As flavors collide in the soft, sugary light.

Grab a fork with glee, let the fun begin,
With every bright bite, we're taken to win.
The kitchen's alive with the songs of delight,
Where the silliness bubbles, as day turns to night.

Crumbs scatter joyfully, we're all in the game,
Each sweetened misstep, a quirky claim to fame.
Sprinkles on top like stars in the sky,
Wondrous creations that make spirits fly.

So cherish the sweetness, and giggles galore,
With crusts made of laughter, we always want more.
As warmth wraps around in a sugary maze,
Each slice of pure bliss, in whipped cream, we gaze.

A Symphony of Citrus Crescendo

With zesty notes ringing, a playful allure,
Citrus serenades, sweet moments secure.
Whipping up joy, a marvelous tune,
As cookies and pies dance beneath the bright moon.

We gather together, a chorus of cheer,
With spoons full of mischief and laughter sincere.
Tartness and sweetness, a rhythmic delight,
In the symphony crafted, we all feel just right.

Every slice tells tales of silly old lore,
As calories vanish, we always want more.
Stuffed with affection, our hearts take a spin,
A joyful explosion, let the fun begin!

So join in the revelry, bring friends for the ride,
In the citrus crescendo, we bask side by side.
With a wink and a nod, life's sweetness we sway,
In this melody of happiness, we play.

Sweet Sunshine Encased

In the kitchen, a dance unfolds,
With zesty scents, a tale retold.
A citrus twist, oh what a craze,
Rolling laughter in sunny rays.

Crust so flaky, it makes us spin,
Whisking dreams beneath our skin.
A sprinkle here, a giggle there,
Joyous chaos fills the air.

Jars of zest split with delight,
Taste buds twirling, oh what a sight!
Slipping on smiles, we share a slice,
Bubbling joy is oh-so-nice!

So come on over, don't be shy,
With empty plates, our spirits fly.
In each bite, a sunny cheer,
Savor the laughter, hold it dear.

Tangles of Butter and Joy

Butter's melting, the mixer spins,
Laughter bubbles where the fun begins.
Sugar dances, twirls, and sings,
While lemon giggles, joy it brings.

A splash of zest in the mixing bowl,
Kneading dough to fill the soul.
Rolling pins are twirling round,
Joyful messes all abound.

Crust so crisp, a golden hue,
Tickling taste buds, just for you.
Whisk the woes away today,
As happiness bakes where we play.

Meringue on top, we can't forget,
A fluffy crown, we're all set.
With each bite, we laugh and cheer,
In this kitchen, love's sincere.

Memories Served with a Zing

A sizzle here, a pop and pour,
Sweet aromas fill the floor.
Whisking humor with a spoon,
Baking memories, afternoon.

Zesty nibbles take the stage,
Each bite is fun, flipping the page.
Citrus giggles roll with glee,
In this world, we're wild and free.

Sliced and served, a treat divine,
Every crumb says, "You are mine!"
Filling hearts, oh what a fling,
With each laugh, we hear the zing.

So gather round, let's take a bite,
Our joyful feast, it feels so right.
In every morsel, smiles are found,
In this chaos, love abounds.

Slice of Laughter

A slice of joy upon our plate,
With sprinkles bright, we celebrate.
Giggles bubble, pastry's light,
As we gather for a bite.

Crust so golden, flaky thin,
Let the laughter now begin.
Spoon to fork, we share the fun,
In our hearts, we all are one.

Zesty twirls in every chew,
Sweet surprise, it feels so new.
Each giggle echoes through the room,
With every slice, we cast away gloom.

So raise your glasses, toast the cheer,
To memories made, so precious, dear.
In this moment, laughter spreads,
With each slice, our joy embeds.

Dollop of Cheer

A dollop here, a splash of fun,
Baking joy until we're done.
Creamy dreams and zesty glee,
Frolicking with our pastry spree.

Whipped and swirled, a cloud of light,
Sprinkling smiles, what a sight!
Laughter echoes from bowl to pan,
In this kitchen, we all can.

Mixing memories, sweet and bright,
With every taste, hearts take flight.
A cheerful scoop, a sprinkle bold,
Stories shared, together told.

So come and savor, friends unite,
In this delight, our spirits bright.
With laughter served and joy so near,
Let's relish this delightful cheer.

Sweet Embrace Wrapped in Crust

In a crust so golden and bright,
Sugar dances, what a delight.
Whipped cream clouds, a frothy tune,
Baked with laughter, we swoon at noon.

Fruits that giggle, tease, and roll,
A zesty bite that fills the soul.
Spoons collide, we crave and share,
With each sweet morsel, joys declare.

Every slice a playful tease,
Sticky fingers, spread with ease.
Joyful crumbs and blissful bites,
Dancing dreams of sugary nights.

Grinning wide, we take a chance,
In dessert's arms, we spin and prance.
Mirthful moments, laughter flows,
In this treat, our happiness grows.

Vibrations of Joy in a Dessert

Beneath the crust, a symphony,
A sweet surprise, an harmony.
Laughter bubbles, flavors unite,
Each savory slice, a pure delight.

In every bite, a giggle waits,
Filling hearts, shoving out fates.
Let's indulge in playful cheer,
With each new spoonful, we draw near.

Twirling spoons in fruity dreams,
Like sunshine bouncing off moonbeams.
Monkeys swing from cherry trees,
Squeezing joy between the tease.

With smirks and grins, we matter not,
In this dessert, we connect a lot.
Bring on the scoop, the waves of glee,
In this dish, we're wild and free.

Roaming through Fields of Flavor

On fields of sweetness, we do roam,
Beneath the sun, we find our home.
A splash of zest, a dash of cheer,
Every morsel whispers, 'Come near!'

Chasing giggles through the custard,
Finding joy in every mustered.
Whirling spoons that twinkle bright,
As flavors join in pure delight.

Butter hills and sugar streams,
Our laughter flows in whipped cream dreams.
Each slice is like a festival,
With joyful bites that are magical.

In this vast land of tasty tease,
We nibble slow, we laugh with ease.
Joy unfolds with every taste,
In fields of flavor, we're never faced.

Daffodils and Dessert Confections

Sweet confections bloom like flowers,
Petals swirling, how the joy towers.
Frosted stems and buttery leaves,
Giggles grow where laughter weaves.

Flavors burst with every bite,
Crisp delights take flight at night.
Marigold dreams and tarts so bright,
In every chew, we find our light.

With smiles as wide as the sky,
Each sugary bloom makes us high.
Chasing tastes in a carnival,
We twirl around, feeling it all.

From bright daffodils to sweet cream,
This is life; it feels like a dream.
Together we savor, unafraid,
In desserts, our laughter's displayed.

www.ingramcontent.com/pod-product-compliance
Ingram Content Group UK Ltd.
Pitfield, Milton Keynes, MK11 3LW, UK
UKHW030057220225
455389UK00006B/51